be easy
dayhikes
Grand Canyon

Ron Adkison

FALCON®

HELENA, MONTANA

⩗FALCON GUIDE®

Falcon® Publishing is continually expanding its list of recreational guidebooks. All books include detailed descriptions, accurate maps, and all information necessary for enjoyable trips. You can order extra copies of this book and get information and prices for other Falcon books by writing Falcon, P.O. Box 1718, Helena, MT 59624 or calling toll free 1-800-582-2665. Also, please ask for a free copy of our current catalog. Visit our web site at http:\\www.falconguide.com

CAUTION

Outdoor recreational activities are by their very nature potentially hazardous. All participants in such activities must assume responsibility for their own actions and safety. The information contained in this guidebook cannot replace sound judgment and good decision-making skills, which help reduce risk exposure, nor does the scope of this book allow for disclosure of all the potential hazards and risks involved in such activities.

Learn as much as possible about the outdoor recreational activities in which you participate, prepare for the unexpected, and be cautious. The reward will be a safer and more enjoyable experience.

♻ Text pages printed on recycled paper.

Contents

The Hikes

Map Legend

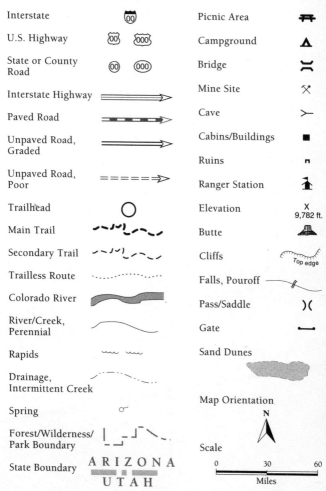

Interstate	
U.S. Highway	
State or County Road	
Interstate Highway	
Paved Road	
Unpaved Road, Graded	
Unpaved Road, Poor	
Trailhead	
Main Trail	
Secondary Trail	
Trailless Route	
Colorado River	
River/Creek, Perennial	
Rapids	
Drainage, Intermittent Creek	
Spring	
Forest/Wilderness/ Park Boundary	
State Boundary	ARIZONA UTAH

Picnic Area	
Campground	
Bridge	
Mine Site	
Cave	
Cabins/Buildings	
Ruins	
Ranger Station	
Elevation	X 9,782 ft.
Butte	
Cliffs	Top edge
Falls, Pouroff	
Pass/Saddle	)(
Gate	
Sand Dunes	

Map Orientation

N

Scale

0   30   60
Miles

Overview Map
Grand Canyon National Park

Introduction

Although thousands of backpackers flock to Grand Canyon National Park each year, many more thousands of visitors don't have the time or desire to undertake a multiday backpack trip below the canyon rim. Luckily, the park offers many excellent day hiking opportunities, and some of the park trails are suitable for novice hikers, even families with small children. Unlike backpacking in the Grand Canyon, day hiking is free and requires no permits.

This indispensable guide to the canyon's best easy day hikes is an abridged version of the comprehensive trail guide *Hiking Grand Canyon National Park*. It is the first and only book dedicated exclusively to day hiking trails in the Grand Canyon. For visitors on a tight schedule or anyone wishing to take a short walk on the park's excellent trails, this book allows readers to quickly and easily choose hikes best suited to their abilities, goals, and time constraints.

The seventeen day hikes described in this book range in length from less than 1 mile to 9.7 miles long, although most hikes average between 2 and 3 miles. Most hikes follow plateau-top trails with minimal elevation gain and loss. Also included are longer plateau-top day hikes that will satisfy more serious hikers who are budgeting time and energy. Since no book of day hikes in the Grand Canyon would be complete without a few hikes below the Canyon rim, some of the "easier" inner canyon day hikes are included here for energetic and fit hikers who wish to sample the canyon's inner depths. All hikes in this book are round-trip hikes, tracing well-defined trails that are easy to follow. Most of these trails lead to dramatic vista points.

For more information about Grand Canyon National Park and its network of trails, contact:

Grand Canyon National Park
P.O. Box 129
Grand Canyon, AZ 86023
(520) 638-7888

Ranking the Hikes

Plateau-Top Hikes

Easiest
Rim Trail
Bright Angel Point
Cape Royal
Cliff Spring
Shoshone Point
Cape Final
Transept Trail
Bill Hall Trail to Monument Point
Ken Patrick Trail
Widforss Trail
Most Difficult Uncle Jim Trail

Hikes Below The Rim

Easiest
Bright Angel Trail to Mile-and-a-half
   Resthouse
North Kaibab Trail to Supai Tunnel
North Bass Trail to Muav Cabin
South Kaibab Trail to Cedar Ridge
Hermit Trail to Santa Maria Spring
Most Difficult Hermits Rest to Dripping Spring

Maps

A variety of good maps show the trails of Grand Canyon National Park, and I recommend two for users of this book.

The first is the Trails Illustrated Grand Canyon National Park topographic map, which shows all the trails in the park from Lees Ferry at River Mile 1 to River Mile 173 near Tuckup Canyon. Trails Illustrated maps are available at many stores and gas stations in communities adjacent to the park; at the Grand Canyon National Park Visitor Center; at Babbitt's General Store on the South Rim; at the general store on the North Rim; and at the North Rim Country Store on the Kaibab Plateau. To order Trails Illustrated maps from the visitor center by mail, call 1-800-858-2808.

The second map I recommend is particularly useful for navigating forest roads on the Kaibab Plateau. It is the North Kaibab District Map of the Kaibab National Forest. You can get Kaibab National Forest maps at the Tusayan Ranger Station, a short distance north of the town of Tusayan, near the south entrance to the park; at the North Kaibab Ranger Station in Fredonia, Arizona; and at the Kaibab Plateau Visitor Center at Jacob Lake, Arizona.

The U.S. Geological Survey and Earthwalk Press also put out good maps of the canyon area. These maps are available at Babbitt's General Store on the South Rim.

Leave No Trace

The desert landscape of the Grand Canyon appears deceptively durable. Actually, it is very fragile. Once damaged, the desert recovers slowly and may not heal completely in your lifetime, if at all. Soils in the Grand Canyon are thin to nonexistent, and plants and desert creatures have evolved a delicate balance of survival. The simple acts of walking off the trail (even for a short distance), crushing plants, or moving rocks disrupt the balance that desert plants and animals have achieved. Taking shortcuts and excavating earth at campsites hasten erosion of the thin soil cover, reducing and, in some instances, eliminating habitat. Shortcutting trails can lead to the eventual destruction of a good (perhaps unmaintained) trail.

Most Grand Canyon hikers have long since learned to employ no-trace practices. Along most of the canyon's trails you seldom will find trash, food scraps, or discarded items. Happily, hikers rarely leave soap suds in precious water sources, evidence of illegal campfires, or signs of unnecessary excavations or alterations. Hikers who wish to be environmentally sensitive should consider the following ideas for no-trace travel as guidelines for preserving the wilderness resource—not only for the canyon's native inhabitants, but also for those who follow in your footsteps.

Three FalconGuide Principles of Leave No Trace
- *Leave with everything you brought with you*
- *Leave no sign of your visit*
- *Leave the landscape as you found it*

Manage Camp Waste

Garbage and food scraps attract animals and insects. Pack out your garbage and leftover food scraps with the rest of your trash.

Deposit human waste at least 200 feet from campsites, trails, water sources, and drainages. Choose a spot with organic soil and dig a cat hole 6 to 8 inches deep, covering the waste with soil. Do not bury or burn your toilet paper. Fires from burning toilet paper have devastated parts of the Canyon; Deer Creek and Hance Creek are examples. *You must pack out all used toilet paper in the Grand Canyon.* Plastic zipper bags are useful for this.

Stay on the Trail

The passage of too many feet creates a lasting trail in the Grand Canyon desert, whether it be from campsite to water source or an off-trail route that can evolve into a trail. Use established trails where they are available. Your boot tracks in trailless areas will encourage others to follow.

Avoid Cryptobiotic Soil Crust

In some areas of the Grand Canyon you will find large areas of soil covered by a black or gray lumpy crust. This cryptobiotic crust is a delicate assemblage of mosses, lichens, blue-green algae, and fungi forming a protective layer against wind and water erosion. The crust aids in the soil's absorption and retention of moisture, allowing larger plants to gain a foothold. The passage of a single hiker can destroy this fragile crust, which may take twenty-five years or longer to develop. In areas covered by cryptobiotic soil crust, hikers must stick to established trails.

Respect Archaeological and Historical Sites

Evidence of ancient cultures and prospectors-turned-tour-guides abounds on Grand Canyon trails. Indeed, all inner canyon trails except the South Kaibab Trail have evolved from routes used by ancient inhabitants that were later improved upon by nineteenth-century prospectors. Along some trails you may encounter archaeological and historical ruins and artifacts. Granaries, rock art, ruins of dwellings, potsherds, the gray ash and charcoal of mescal roasting pits, prospectors' cabins, and mining and camp relics are among the cultural resources hikers may find in the Grand Canyon backcountry.

The majority of archaeological sites date back to between A.D. 1050 and A.D. 1200, a time when the Anasazi people widely occupied the Grand Canyon region. Ancient granaries and ruins are very fragile, so restrain the urge to enter them and climb on their stone walls. Walk carefully around the slopes that support these structures. Ruins may be the highlight of a hike, but they are inappropriate places to camp or eat meals. Food crumbs and garbage may attract rodents that could then nest in the site and damage it.

Pigments of ancient pictographs are easily destroyed by skin oils. Restrain the urge to touch them, particularly handprint pictographs. Never add your own graffiti to irreplaceable rock art panels. If you happen upon an archaeological site where artifacts remain, you may photograph them, but if you pick up or rearrange objects you may be destroying an important link to the past. Once an artifact is removed or disturbed, it becomes merely an object with little meaning to archaeologists.

Keep in mind that these nonrenewable resources offer archaeologists insights into past ways of life in the Grand Canyon and can be easily disturbed and damaged by curious hikers. Although federal and state laws protect cultural resources, ultimately it depends on each of us to walk softly and treat these resources with the respect they deserve. Excavation and stabilization of many sites has yet to take place. Although you are likely to encounter many such sites on Grand Canyon trails, this book will not lead you to them, preserving for hikers the sense of discovery.

Shuttle Services

West Rim Shuttle

West Rim Drive is closed to private vehicles to relieve congestion from late May through September. During that time, the West Rim Shuttle operates daily, running every 15 minutes from 7:30 a.m. to sunset. There is no fee. You can board the brown-and-tan bus at the West Rim Interchange bus stop, adjacent to Bright Angel Lodge and the Bright Angel Trailhead. This shuttle is useful for hikers taking Hikes 4-6.

Kaibab Shuttle

The Kaibab Hikers' Shuttle connects the Grand Canyon Village area with the South Kaibab trailhead for a small fee. The bus departs from the front porch of Bright Angel Lodge at 6:30 a.m., 8:30 a.m., and 11:30 a.m., and from Maswik Lodge at 6:50 a.m., 8:50 a.m., and 11:50 a.m. daily. The bus leaves the South Kaibab trailhead at 7:10 a.m., 9:10 a.m., and 12:10 p.m. This shuttle serves hikers taking Hike 2.

Park plans eventually call for the closure of the South Kaibab trailhead to private vehicles, at least during the peak season. At that time, a free shuttle will offer access from Grand Canyon Village to the trailhead. Check with the Backcountry Reservations Office (BRO) for current information and schedules.

North Rim Shuttle

On the North Rim, a hikers' shuttle, available for a small fee, departs from Grand Canyon Lodge and takes hikers to the often full North Kaibab trailhead parking lot. The shuttle runs from 6 a.m. to 8 p.m. daily when the North Rim is in full swing, mid-May through mid-October. This shuttle can be useful for hikers taking Hikes 11-13.

Items Every Hiker Should Carry

- 2 quarts of water per person
- First-aid kit including bandages, moleskin, lip balm, and sunscreen
- Signal mirror
- Food
- Map
- Sweater or parka
- Rain gear or windproof parka
- Hat with brim
- Lightweight and durable hiking boots
- Toilet paper and resealable plastic bag for packing out used toilet paper, a National Park Service requirement

The South Rim

When most people envision the Grand Canyon, images of its South Rim come to mind. After all, the South Rim is the most photographed part of the canyon, and calendars, postcards, and magazine articles have planted its panoramas in our minds. The vast majority of park visitors come to the South Rim for ample reasons. The South Rim offers an abundance of visitor services; it is easily accessible; and its vistas are among the finest in the park.

Panoramas of the Grand Canyon unfold to their greatest dimensions from the South Rim. Most often, air quality in the desert Southwest, including the Grand Canyon, is among the best in the nation. Night sky viewing is excellent. A visual range of 243 miles has been observed at the Grand Canyon, and it is not unusual to clearly see plateaus and the dome of Navajo Mountain in southern Utah from the South Rim, more than 100 miles distant. Hikers come to the South Rim in large numbers for many of these same reasons, plus the fact that most trailheads are easily accessible via paved roads. And there are more trails below the South Rim than elsewhere in the national park.

Unfortunately for hikers, so much of the South Rim is claimed by roads and other developments that there are few opportunities for day hikes there. Yet there are two notable exceptions: the excellent Rim Trail and the closed road to Shoshone Point. Most South Rim day hikers descend into the canyon and, of course, hike back out. Most hikers do not seem to mind this down and up trek, though, since the magnetic attraction of the inner canyon lures tens of thousands of day hikers onto South Rim trails each year.

Camping and Lodging

The South Rim is home to two fee campgrounds and an RV park. The 320-site Mather Campground, featuring water, toilets, tables, fire pits, and grills, is located south of Babbitt's General Store in Grand Canyon Village. The campground is available on a first-come, first-served basis from December 1 through March 1. At other times, you must book sites well in advance. (Phone 1-800-365-2267 for reservations.) The 84-site Trailer Village adjacent to Mather Campground has RV hookups.

Desert View Campground, with water, tables, toilets, fire pits, and grills, is a 50-site campground on the South Rim at Desert View, 26 miles east of Grand Canyon Village on East Rim Drive. Sites are available on a first-come, first-served basis only.

Lodging is available in the lodges at Grand Canyon Village; make reservations well in advance by phoning (303) 297-2757. Visitors may also stay in the communities of Tusayan, Cameron, Flagstaff, and Williams, Arizona.

Access

The South Rim is open year-round and can be reached from Interstate 40 in the south. From Williams, Arizona, drive north on Arizona Highway 64 for 59 miles to reach the village. From Flagstaff, follow U.S. Highway 180 and AZ 64 for 78 miles. From the east, find the junction of AZ

64 and US 89 at Cameron, on the Navajo Indian Reservation. Cameron is located 82 miles south of Page, Arizona, 58.3 miles south of the US 89/89A junction, and 16 miles south of the US 89/160 junction. Grand Canyon Village can be reached from Cameron by following AZ 64 west for 57 miles.

1
SHOSHONE POINT

General description: An easy day hike to a glorious South Rim viewpoint.

Distance: 2 miles round-trip.

Difficulty: Easy.

Average hiking time: 40 to 60 minutes round-trip.

Type of trail: Dirt road.

Trailhead elevation: 7,190 feet.

High point: 7,300 feet.

Elevation gain: 110 feet.

Water availability: None available.

Optimum season: April through November.

Topo maps: USGS Phantom Ranch quad; Trails Illustrated Grand Canyon National Park; Earthwalk Grand Canyon National Park.

Finding the trailhead: Find this unsigned trailhead along the north side of East Rim Drive, 3.5 miles east of the Arizona Highway 64/Village Loop Road junction and 1.3 miles east of the prominently signed Yaki Point turnoff. If you are approaching from the east via Desert View, note your odometer reading at the Grandview Point turnoff. You pass a picnic area on the north side of the road 2.7 miles west of the Grandview Point turnoff and reach the Shoshone Point Road and small parking area 6.3 miles west of the turnoff to Grandview Point.

Shoshone Point

Key points:
0.0   Shoshone Point Road.
1.0   Shoshone Point.

The hike: If time and energy allow you to hike only a few short trails on the South Rim, the trip to Shoshone Point, combining a walk through cool pine forests with truly dramatic vistas of the eastern Grand Canyon, should be at the top of your list. Your solitude may be disrupted at times at the point, however. The picnic area at the road's end is an occasionally popular spot for weddings, family gatherings, and other festivities. The site is available for day use by fee and permit from May 15 to October 15. Contact Park Headquarters at (520) 638-7761 for the information sheet on Shoshone Point. Before and after those dates, you'll likely have Shoshone Point to yourself.

The majority of South Rim viewpoints offer easy and short (yet often crowded and noisy) hikes from their paved parking lots. Seldom does a visitor enjoy quiet solitude when gazing across the vast depths of the Grand Canyon. Shoshone Point is a notable exception. Anyone willing to walk a 1-mile, nearly level dirt road will enjoy the opportunity to contemplate this great canyon in relative solitude. Perched high on the South Rim on a point of land dividing Grapevine and Cremation canyons, Shoshone Point offers one of the finest vistas available from the South Rim.

Begin your walk at the locked gate on the Shoshone Point Road. The road rises imperceptibly up a shallow draw beneath the shade of tall ponderosa pines. Gambel oaks and occasional piñons and junipers mix into the ranks of the pine forest. Typical of both rims of the canyon, the forest signals your approach to the rim. The pines quickly diminish and are supplanted by a woodland of piñon and juniper. Shortly after entering this woodland, the road edges close to the east rim of the point, and soon you reach the loop at the road's end, where you find picnic tables, a large fire pit, fire grills, portable toilets, and garbage cans, facilities well-used by visitors who have acquired permits to drive the dirt road in season (see above).

A well-worn path ascends north beyond here, then descends another 150 yards among gnarled piñons and over slabs of Kaibab Limestone out to the point, where an unobstructed vista of the Grand Canyon unfolds, far from the crowds, noisy buses, and exhaust fumes of other South Rim viewpoints. Upcanyon to the east you can see the foaming torrent of Hance Rapids, but elsewhere the river is blocked from your view by the Tapeats Sandstone rim of the inner gorge. On the skyline beyond the rapids is Desert View Watchtower, and your eyes follow the east rim of the canyon past the towering walls of the Palisades of the Desert to the distant Marble Platform and the Echo Cliffs.

Part of that view is obscured by the pyramidal crag of Vishnu Temple, one of the canyon's most striking peaks. From Powell Plateau in the northwest, past Point Sublime to Cape Royal and Wotans Throne in the northeast, the forest-fringed North Rim and an incredible array of colorful buttes, mesas, and spires spread out before you.

Virtually at your feet, the broad, dry wash of the east fork of Cremation Creek winds northwest and disappears into its Tapeats Sandstone narrows above Granite Gorge. The switchbacks of the South Kaibab Trail through the Redwall Limestone are clearly visible west of Cremation's broad desert basin. Clear Creek canyon, with its own tortuous Vishnu Gorge, winds northeast beyond the invisible river, gathering waters from many-fingered canyons that reach up to the forested rim of Walhalla Plateau.

Lying far below is the wash of Boulder Creek, north of the point. To the east are the depths of Grapevine Creek, one of the South Rim's most extensive canyons. Other prominent features below the South Rim and east of the point include Horseshoe Mesa, Sinking Ship, Coronado Butte, and the distant red buttes of Escalante and Cardenas looming above the Tanner Trail.

While you are on the point, you may notice a grove of Douglas-fir clinging to the foot of the Kaibab Limestone cliff below the picnic area. More of these Canadian Zone trees can be seen to the west, occupying the Toroweap Formation slopes westward toward Yaki Point, between drought-tolerant bands of piñon and juniper. After enjoying the tremendous vistas, retrace your steps to the trailhead.

2
SOUTH KAIBAB TRAIL TO CEDAR RIDGE

General description: A view-packed half-day hike below the South Rim, following one of the most popular trails in the Grand Canyon.

Distance: 2.8 miles round-trip.

Difficulty: Moderate.

Average hiking time: 3 hours round-trip.

Type of trail: Maintained; excellent condition.

Trailhead elevation: 7,200 feet.

Low point: 6,050 feet.

Elevation loss: 1,150 feet.

Water availability: None available.

Optimum seasons: March though June; September through November.

Topo maps: USGS Phantom Ranch quad; Trails Illustrated Grand Canyon National Park; Earthwalk Bright Angel Trail or Grand Canyon National Park.

Finding the trailhead: Find this well-signed trailhead by driving 1.1 miles east on East Rim Drive from the Arizona Highway 64/Village Loop Road junction to the Yaki Point turnoff, also signed for Kaibab Trail. Follow this spur road north for 0.3 mile, then turn left where the sign points to the trailhead. After another 0.3 mile, you reach the trailhead parking lot. Seasonal drinking water, toilets, garbage collec-

South Kaibab Trail to Cedar Ridge

tion, and a pay telephone are available here. If you are approaching from the east, follow East Rim Dr. west from the Desert View Entrance Station for 20.8 miles to reach the Yaki Point turnoff.

Note: Due to congestion and overcrowding at the South Kaibab trailhead, this area may be closed to private vehicles in the near future. Hikers must then use the Kaibab Shuttle to reach the trailhead. (For more information on shuttles, check with the Backcountry Reservations Office for current schedules.)

Key points:
0.0   South Kaibab Trailhead.
1.4   Cedar Ridge.

The hike: Much like the Bright Angel Trail, the South Kaibab Trail is a must-do for Grand Canyon visitors wishing to see the canyon from the inside out. Hikers flock to this excellent trail in a steady stream for much of the year, and the majority of trail users are day hikers making the rewarding trip to Cedar Ridge. A continuum of tremendous vistas unfold with every step of the way, and interpretive signs along the trail offer insights into Grand Canyon geology. The trail—the most popular day hike in the park—is moderately steep and shadeless. Unlike the Bright Angel Trail, no drinking water is available. Mule trains returning from Phantom Ranch use the trail daily. When you encounter mules, step quietly off the trail and allow them to pass.

From the trailhead parking lot, follow the trail north past the mule corrals for several yards to the piñon and juniper-clad South Rim. Here, next to a pay telephone and interpretive signboard, the South Kaibab Trail begins its plunge into the Grand Canyon. A series of wide switchbacks lead down through the gray cliff band of Kaibab Limestone at a moderate grade. In winter, when the route is covered with snow or ice, the wide trail is still reasonably safe and easy to follow.

At the foot of the Kaibab cliff, hikers traverse north upon the steep red slopes of the Toroweap Formation. Here piñons and junipers reappear, along with an occasional Douglas-fir in sheltered recesses. Pipe Creek canyon lies far below the trail, and shady alcoves at its head also support Douglas-fir, growing in an extensive grove.

Where the trail rounds the shoulder of Cedar Ridge, you reach the sparkling Coconino Sandstone. Follow the rocky trail steadily downhill, switching back from one side of the ridge to the other. O'Neill Butte, capped by a block of red Esplanade Sandstone, looms ahead as you stroll down the red slopes of Hermit Shale to the broad, piñon- and juniper-studded platform of Cedar Ridge at 6,050 feet. Soon you will pass the solar dehydrating toilets and reach a dramatic vista point, the goal of most day hikers on the trail.

A boot-worn trail leads 300 yards northwest to the point of the ridge, which affords even broader panoramas. Pipe Creek canyon lies far below to the west, and one can visually trace the course of the Tonto Trail as it traverses that creek's basin en route to Indian Garden. The Devil's Corkscrew on the Bright Angel Trail is visible as it descends from the hanging valley of Garden Creek into the dark Vishnu Schist hallway of lower Pipe Creek.

The broad, blackbrush-studded basin of Cremation Creek spreads out below and to the east of your vantage point. Far beyond rises the barrier wall of the Palisades of the Desert, and Desert View Watchtower can be seen capping the eastern end of the South Rim. The forest-fringed North Rim provides a backdrop for your canyon vista. To the northeast, the erosion-isolated mesa of Wotans Throne and the slender spire of Vishnu Temple rise in bold relief.

From Cedar Ridge, backtrack to the trailhead.

3
BRIGHT ANGEL TRAIL TO MILE-AND-A-HALF RESTHOUSE

General description: A very scenic half-day hike below the South Rim along the Grand Canyon's most popular trail.

Distance: 3 miles round-trip.

Difficulty: Moderate.

Average hiking time: 2 to 3 hours round-trip.

Type of trail: Maintained; excellent condition.

Trailhead elevation: 6,820 feet.

Low point: 5,700 feet.

Elevation loss: 1,120 feet.

Water availability: Available May through September at Mile-and-a-half Resthouse.

Optimum seasons: March through June; September through November.

Topo maps: USGS Grand Canyon quad; Trails Illustrated Grand Canyon National Park; Earthwalk Bright Angel Trail or Grand Canyon National Park.

Finding the trailhead: The Bright Angel Trail begins just west of Bright Angel Lodge on the South Rim at the West Rim Drive interchange. No parking is available at the trailhead. Hikers must park at either the public parking lot adjacent to Maswik Lodge, 0.2 mile south of Bright Angel Lodge, or in one of the large parking areas south of the railroad tracks between Bright Angel Lodge and the train depot.

To reach the Bright Angel Lodge area and the West

Bright Angel Trail to Mile-and-a-half Resthouse

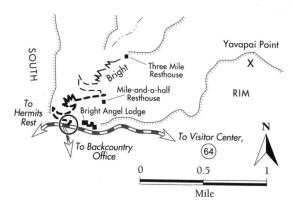

Rim Dr. interchange, follow the Village Loop Road, which begins at the Arizona Highway 64/East Rim Drive intersection, for 2.75 miles to a Y junction in Grand Canyon Village. Bear right at that junction onto a one-way road, prominently signed for El Tovar and Bright Angel Lodge. Follow the road past the train depot and hotel complex for another 0.6 mile to the West Rim Dr. interchange. Here, turn left (south) to reach the public parking areas within another 0.2 mile.

Key points:
0.0 Bright Angel Trailhead.
1.5 Mile-and-a-half Resthouse.

The hike: The Bright Angel Trail is the most popular trail in the park, and one of the most beautiful. Splendid vistas, an excellent, well-groomed trail, and a shady resthouse located just far enough below the rim for hikers to gain the feel and appreciate the dimensions of the inner canyon combine to make this hike an excellent choice for first-time Grand Canyon hikers.

Although water is seasonally available at the resthouse, breaks in the water pipeline occasionally occur. Thus hikers are strongly advised to carry their own water. Mule trains use this trail each day to descend into the canyon en route to Plateau Point and Phantom Ranch. As a result of this heavy downhill traffic, the trail is rougher than the South Kaibab Trail and the tread has developed a corrugated surface.

The trail begins immediately north of the West Rim interchange, a short distance west of the Bright Angel Lodge complex. Follow the trail as it descends below the rim, avoiding two right-branching spurs of the Rim Trail within the first several yards. Beyond the first switchback, you pass through a tunnel carved into the Kaibab Limestone. Look for a pictograph panel, believed to be of Havasupai origin, just above the trail beyond the tunnel. Although the Bright Angel Trail follows a canyon route, excellent views are nevertheless enjoyed from the beginning. Far below lies Indian Garden, an oasis surrounded by the blackbrush flats of the Tonto Platform. The Plateau Point Trail, nearly as wide as a road, appears as a white scar across the Tonto Platform, beyond Indian Garden.

The Bright Angel Fault, a prominent feature in this part of the Grand Canyon, is one of many faults in the canyon that have altered the generally flat-lying layers of sedimentary rock. It stretches northeast from the Coconino Plateau to the Kaibab Plateau. Garden Creek below you and the distant trough of Bright Angel Canyon were eroded along this zone of shattered rock. The cliffs that bound the headwaters amphitheater of Garden Creek are noticeably offset by movement along the fault. The cliffs to the west were uplifted nearly 200 feet relative to the cliffs east of the canyon. The resulting break in the cliff bands has been used by humans for centuries to reach the inner canyon.

After two long switchbacks through the Toroweap Formation, you pass through a second short tunnel, then reach the Coconino Sandstone. Here a series of short, moderately steep switchbacks leads down through the fault-controlled break in the Coconino cliff. Garden Creek's drainage has carved a steep gully in this break, through which the trail descends among a jumble of shattered blocks. A scattering of Douglas-fir appears in the cool, shady microclimate that prevails at the base of the gully.

Beyond the switchbacks, a steadily descending traverse of steep, red Hermit Shale slopes leads down to Mile-and-a-half Resthouse, tucked away in a shady recess. Seasonal drinking water, toilets, and an emergency telephone are available here. From the resthouse, you can visually trace the cavernous course of Bright Angel Creek, carved along the arrow-straight line of the Bright Angel Fault, as it reaches far back toward the North Rim. An array of varicolored buttes and towers, including Sumner Butte, Cheops Pyramid, and Brahma Temple, punctuate the middle distance.

Return to the rim the way you came.

4
RIM TRAIL

General description: The best easy hike on the South Rim, offering a continuum of dramatic canyon views.

Distance: Variable, up to 9.7 miles one way.

Difficulty: Easy in short segments; moderate if the entire trail is followed.

Average hiking times: Variable.

Type of trail: Paved from Yavapai Point to Maricopa Point; unmaintained, in fair condition, from Maricopa Point to Hermits Rest.

Trailhead elevation: Variable, depending on starting point; ranging from 7,065 feet to 6,640 feet.

Elevation gain and loss: Minimal.

Water availability: None available.

Optimum season: April through October.

Topo maps: USGS Phantom Ranch and Grand Canyon quads; Trails Illustrated Grand Canyon National Park; Earthwalk Grand Canyon National Park (entire trail shown only on Earthwalk map).

Finding the trailhead: This trail can be reached from twelve different access points. From east to west they are: Yavapai Point; the visitor center; the El Tovar/Bright Angel Lodge complex; Bright Angel Trailhead/West Rim Interchange; Trailview Overlook; Maricopa Point; Powell Memorial; Hopi Point; Mohave Point; The Abyss overlook; Pima Point; and Hermits Rest. Hikers on the Rim Trail usually follow the trail for a short distance from one of these access points, then either backtrack to their cars or take advantage of the park's free shuttle bus system.

Perhaps the best way to hike segments of the Rim Trail is to park in the public parking areas near Bright Angel Lodge (south of West Rim Interchange), and either begin hiking from there and returning via a shuttle bus, or ride a bus to another access point and hike back to your car. To reach that parking area, follow driving directions for Hike 3. When you enter the national park, be sure to obtain a copy of *The Guide*, the park's information newspaper, which shows a map of the trail and gives information regarding shuttle buses and bus stop locations.

Key points:
0.0 Yavapai Point.
0.8 Junction with trail to visitor center; continue straight ahead.
1.4 Enter lodge complex.
1.9 Bright Angel Trailhead/West Rim Interchange; continue straight ahead alongside West Rim Drive.
3.0 Maricopa Point, end of paved trail.
3.5 Powell Point, Powell Memorial.
3.8 Hopi Point.
4.6 Mohave Point.
5.7 The Abyss overlook.
8.6 Pima Point.
9.7 Hermits Rest.

Rim Trail

The hike: The scenic Rim Trail is arguably Grand Canyon National Park's finest easy day hike. Nowhere else in the park do Grand Canyon vistas unfold in such breathtaking dimensions. Although the trail often closely follows park roads, segments of the trail (notably, between Yavapai Point and the lodge complex, and between The Abyss and Pima Point) deviate from the course of the road, allowing hikers to enjoy interesting perspectives of the canyon in comparative solitude.

Yavapai Point to the lodge complex, 1.4 miles

From the Yavapai Observation Station, the Rim Trail curves left and follows the edge of the wooded South Rim high above Garden Creek canyon. After 0.8 mile, a signed trail branches left (south), leading 0.4 mile to the park visitor center. The final 0.6 mile of this segment affords fine views into the depths of Garden Creek, past an array of colorful inner canyon buttes, to the bold cliffs and terraces that stair-step up to the distant North Rim. After 1.4 miles you reach the east end of the lodge complex at Verkamp's Curios.

Verkamp's to the Bright Angel Trailhead, 0.5 mile

This flat segment is the busiest part of the trail, passing the historic buildings of Verkamp's Curios, Hopi House (built around the turn of the twentieth century in the Pueblo style), El Tovar Hotel, Bright Angel Lodge, and Kolb Studio. This part of the trail is best suited to visitors browsing the curio shops and art exhibits, and to restaurant and lodge guests. Vistas, as usual along the Rim Trail, are panoramic, affording aerial-like views into the Grand Canyon, including the cottonwood-shaded oasis of Indian Garden far below.

Bright Angel Trailhead to Maricopa Point, 1.1 miles

This segment of the Rim Trail gradually ascends the West Rim to Maricopa Point. As the trail hugs the rim, it affords fine views of hikers far below on the switchbacks of the Bright Angel Trail. You will be joined by many other hikers after passing Trailview Overlook after 0.5 mile. Shortly beyond the Maricopa Point parking area, after 1.1 miles, the pavement ends at Maricopa Point proper.

Maricopa Point to Hermits Rest, 6.7 miles

Best done in two or three shorter segments for a leisurely hike, the Rim Trail section between Maricopa Point and Hermits Rest is perhaps the most dramatic and interesting part of its route. The unpaved trail is often narrow and much less frequently used than previous segments. Exercise care, since the trail often clings to steep slopes and the very edge of plunging cliffs.

From Maricopa Point, the trail leads past the old buildings of the Lost Orphan Mine, a rich uranium mine dating back to the 1950s uranium boom. About 200 yards beyond the mine, you reach another parking area and the very short spur trail to Powell Point, offering another fine canyon panorama and a memorial placed in honor of John Wesley Powell and his epic 1869 expedition down the Colorado River.

The Rim Trail continues on to Hopi Point, after another 0.8 mile. Beyond the point, a new perspective of the canyon unfolds, and vistas stretch far downcanyon to distant Powell Plateau and the dome of Mount Trumbull. Frequent views of the Colorado River far below, including the foaming cauldrons of Granite and Hermit rapids, help illustrate the canyon's immense depth. The sinuous Tonto Trail is occasionally visible, traversing the desert terrace of the Tonto Platform about 3,500 feet below.

After 1.6 miles the path curves around Mohave Point, then follows the rim far back toward the head of The Abyss. This aptly named void is notable not only for its broad, colorful, 3,000-foot-deep amphitheater, but also for its unusual groves of Douglas-fir, a high elevation conifer common on the Kaibab Plateau but found here only in the coolest microclimates below the South Rim cliffs. Like the Tonto Trail far below, the Rim Trail must detour around the gaping void of The Abyss. The 4 miles from Mohave Point to Pima Point (at 5.6 miles) are long yet spectacular.

The final 1.1-mile leg of the Rim Trail from Pima Point to Hermits Rest affords tremendous views into Hermit Creek canyon and to Hermit and Boucher rapids. Once you reach the Hermits Rest parking area, board the next brown-and-tan bus and return to the West Rim Interchange.

5
HERMITS TRAIL TO SANTA MARIA SPRING

General description: A rewarding day hike below the western reaches of the South Rim.

Distance: 4.6 miles round-trip.

Difficulty: Moderate.

Average hiking time: 3 to 4 hours round-trip.

Type of trail: Unmaintained; generally good condition.

Trailhead elevation: 6,640 feet.

Low point: 5,000 feet.

Elevation loss: 1,640 feet.

Water availability: Santa Maria Spring at 2.25 miles offers a trickling seep, but since water must be treated, bring your own.

Optimum seasons: March through June; September through November.

Topo maps: USGS Grand Canyon quad; Trails Illustrated Grand Canyon National Park; Earthwalk Grand Canyon National Park.

Finding the trailhead: From late May through September, West Rim Drive is closed to private vehicles. During this time, a free shuttle bus offers access to Hermits Rest every 15 minutes from 7:30 a.m. to sunset each day. You can board the brown-and-white buses at the West Rim Dr. interchange.

To find Hermits Rest when West Rim Dr. is open, follow driving directions for Hike 3 to the West Rim Dr. interchange, then proceed straight ahead on West Rim Dr. for 7 miles to the loop at the end of the pavement at Hermits Rest. A sign here points to Hermit Trail parking; follow the dirt spur road for another 0.2 mile down to the trailhead. Drinking water, toilets, garbage collection, a pay telephone, pop machine, snack bar, and curio shop are available at Hermits Rest.

Key points:
0.0   Hermits Rest Trailhead parking area.
1.5   Junction with Waldron Trail; stay right.
1.8   Junction with Dripping Spring Trail; bear right.
2.3   Santa Maria Spring.

The hike: This fine trip follows a trail constructed by the Santa Fe Railroad in 1912 and leads to the shady resthouse at Santa Maria Spring, perched high above the abyss of Hermit Creek canyon. Although the trail was abandoned in 1931 and the tread is generally rougher than the groomed Corridor trails, it remains easy to follow as far as the spring.

The abrupt cliffs of the South Rim have been softened by time below Hermits Rest, and the Hermit Trail takes advantage of this break, as it descends a moderate yet rocky grade through piñon-juniper woodlands below the road's end. After dropping into a shallow draw, the trail switchbacks briefly through the Kaibab Limestone, then begins a southbound traverse over red and gray Toroweap Formation slopes. Piñon and juniper are joined on the trailside slopes by a

Hermits Trail to Santa Maria Spring, Hermits Rest to Dripping Spring

shrub cover of cliffrose, littleleaf mountain mahogany, and sagebrush. Exciting views begin to unfold here, reaching across the gaping red abyss of Hermit Creek canyon to the soaring cliffs that bound the wooded hanging valley of Hermit Basin.

The traverse ends upon reaching the sparkling sandstone of the broken Coconino cliff. Switchbacks ensue, leading steadily downhill over ledges and slabs. Reminiscent of the Grandview Trail, the steeper pitches here are paved with cobbles, allowing the tread to withstand the ravages of erosion. Keep an eye out for fossil reptile tracks on trailside slabs; they are more obvious here than along any other Grand Canyon trail. Mats of scrub live oak join various other shrubs here. Along with abundant piñon and juniper, woodland shrubs and small trees form a drab green veneer that engulfs Hermit Basin and obscures much of the canyon's upper rock layers, lending a softer appearance to the landscape.

After emerging onto the red slopes of Hermit Shale that flank Hermit Basin, the trail begins a straightforward, steep, and rocky descent past the signed junction with the seldom-used Waldron Trail at 5,400 feet. Finally the grade moderates in the wash on the basin floor. At the junction here, at 5,200 feet, turn right. The trail ahead continues west to the Boucher Trail and Dripping Spring (Hike 6).

From the junction, short switchbacks lead down to the crossing of the dry wash, where the trail is funneled between two slickrock pouroffs. The trail ahead descends 250 feet in 0.5 mile, with the aid of a few switchbacks, to the Santa Maria Spring Resthouse. This long, roofed shelter, draped by an arbor of canyon wild grape, offers a welcome refuge from the sun. The spring, however, is a mere trickle. It offers enough water for a drink, but filling a bottle requires a long-term commitment. From the pleasant shade of the resthouse, return the way you came.

6
HERMITS REST TO DRIPPING SPRING

see map on page 36

General description: A rewarding day hike below the South Rim, leading to an aptly named spring.
Distance: 6.6 miles round-trip.
Difficulty: Moderate.
Average hiking time: 4 to 5 hours round-trip.
Type of trail: Unmaintained; generally good condition.
Trailhead elevation: 6,640 feet.
Low point: 5,150 feet.
Elevation gain and loss: +400 feet; -1,600 feet.
Water availability: Dripping Spring (must be treated before drinking); bring your own.
Optimum season: March through November.
Topo maps: USGS Grand Canyon quad; Trails Illustrated Grand Canyon National Park; Earthwalk Grand Canyon National Park.
Finding the trailhead: Follow driving directions for Hike 5. There are two alternative ways to reach the spring: via the

Waldron Trail and via Louis Boucher's original Dripping Spring Trail. Those trails can be reached by following a confusing network of park roads west from the Rowe Well Picnic Area, but they are seldom used. Finding the trailheads takes map-reading skills, as well as driving skills on exceedingly rough and rocky four-wheel-drive roads. Contact the Backcountry Reservations Office for directions if you are determined to use one of those trails.

Key points:
0.0   Hermits Rest Trailhead parking area.
1.5   Junction with Waldron Trail; stay right.
1.8   Junction of Hermit and Dripping Spring trails; bear left.
2.8   Junction with northbound Boucher Trail; stay left.
3.3   Dripping Spring.

The hike: The hike to Dripping Spring via the Hermit Trail is one of the best day trips on the South Rim. The trail offers a good introduction to the nature of Grand Canyon trails, as well as dramatic vistas, and ends at an unusual spring where water rains from the roof of an alcove at the base of the Coconino Sandstone. Hikers should carry ample water for the round trip, since Dripping Spring water must be treated before drinking.

From the Hermits Rest Trailhead parking area, follow the Hermit Trail (see Hike 5), descending 1,450 feet in 1.8 miles and about one hour to Hermit Basin. From the signed junction, bear left toward Dripping Spring and the Boucher Trail. The following mile of trail is an exciting stretch that undulates along the steep slopes of the red Hermit Shale. The trail is, by necessity, funneled between the sheer, 1,200-foot Kaibab–Toroweap–Coconino cliffs above and the 800-foot Supai cliffs below.

With minor undulations, the trail curves into two prominent, shadowed amphitheaters that host a rich woodland of tall, spreading shrubs and small trees, such as pale hoptree, Utah serviceberry, alder-leaf mountain mahogany, Fremont barberry, mock orange, squaw currant, and single-leaf ash. The Supai cliffs at the trail's edge plummet into the narrows of upper Hermit Creek canyon far below, lying in the near-perpetual shade of towering Redwall cliffs. The North Rim, cool and forested, rises in the distance behind innumerable buttes, towers, and terraces.

At length you enter the wooded lower reaches of the Dripping Spring draw, where you meet the northbound Boucher Trail. Bear left at the junction and begin a moderate ascent west up the draw through an open woodland of piñon, juniper, cliffrose, scrub live oak, fragrant ash, apache plume, and other shrubs. The draw ahead appears to dead-end in an amphitheater embraced by bulging, cross-bedded walls of Coconino Sandstone, stained with veils of brown desert varnish. Soon you reach the head of the amphitheater, then curve into its sheltered alcove. Here, beneath the overhanging sandstone walls, you find Dripping Spring.

True to its name, the spring drips from the roof of the alcove, decorated with clumps of maidenhair fern, into a small, rock-framed pool fringed by the nodding blooms of scarlet monkeyflower. Other seeps, also fringed with ferns, emerge from the walls of the alcove, a few feet above the

Coconino Sandstone/Hermit Shale contact zone. Ample shade is cast by the alcove's overhanging walls and by the thickets of shrubs and netleaf hackberry trees that surround it. Coconino cliffs rise 300 to 400 feet above this peaceful locale, where you will likely enjoy the aerial acrobatics of white-throated swifts and violet-green swallows, and perhaps hear the melancholy song of a canyon wren.

Louis Boucher maintained a tent camp and corrals on the bench below the spring from the 1890s to about 1912. Nature has since reclaimed the site, and now the bench hosts the spreading foliage of netleaf hackberry and redbud trees. (No camping is allowed here or elsewhere along the trail). Boucher's original trail continues east through the alcove beyond Dripping Spring, then ascends 800 feet in 1.3 miles to the remote trailhead atop the South Rim.

From Dripping Spring, return the way you came.

The North Rim

The North Rim of the Grand Canyon forms an alluring backdrop to vistas from the South Rim. Its fringe of tall conifers holds the promise of a cool refuge from desert heat and solitude in a wilderness setting. The North Rim has an atmosphere of great remoteness and unspoiled grandeur. It is this remoteness that makes it such a special place.

Separated from the South Rim by only 10 to 12 miles as the crow flies, the North Rim can be reached in two ways: either by hiking 21 miles across the Grand Canyon or by driving 215 miles around it. The North Rim lies at the end of a long, dead-end road that traverses the rich conifer forests and grassy parks of the Kaibab Plateau, many miles from the nearest enclaves of civilization. Though the North Rim receives only one-tenth the number of visitors as the South Rim, fewer roads and visitor services here concentrate use so that places here can seem congested at times.

Canyon overlooks on national park roads at the North Rim are not as abundant as on the South Rim, where it seems every bend in the road presents an incredible vista. As if to compensate for fewer overlooks, North Rim viewpoints afford vistas of the Grand Canyon that are consistently awe-inspiring and overwhelming, even to the most jaded canyoneer. Fringed with forests of pine, fir, spruce, and aspen, North Rim overlooks survey a remarkable landscape of colorful cliffs, bold towers, deep labyrinths, and seemingly barren desert.

FALCON®

BUSINESS REPLY MAIL

FIRST-CLASS MAIL   PERMIT NO. 80   HELENA MT

POSTAGE WILL BE PAID BY THE ADDRESSEE

FALCON PUBLISHING CO INC
PO BOX 1718
HELENA MT   59624-9917

Most North Rim trails are as lonely as the nearby over-looks are congested. Only one maintained trail descends into the Grand Canyon from the North Rim, and this, the North Kaibab Trail, receives the bulk of use here, for good reasons. The North Kaibab is a highly scenic, excellent trail that offers something for everyone, from the visitor out for a stroll to the backpacker plunging into the Grand Canyon's depths.

Numerous trails atop the Kaibab Plateau at the North Rim offer fine day hiking opportunities. These trails are an excellent choice for summer season hikers wishing to avoid the overwhelming heat of the inner canyon, yet still enjoy incomparable views. The North Rim boasts the highest concentration of plateau-top trails in the park. Hikers can spend several days traversing them all, or spend only an hour or two on one of the many rewarding short trails. These trails are easy to follow and are among the best of the Grand Canyon's easy day hikes.

Camping

The 82-site North Rim Campground, open from May 15 through October 15, is the only campground on the North Rim of the Grand Canyon. Facilities in this fee campground include water, tables, toilets, fire pits, and grills. Some sites may be available at your time of arrival, but to ensure you get a site, make reservations by phoning 1-800-365-2267.

Kaibab National Forest is open to at-large camping, and many excellent sites can be found along almost any forest road. Campers must be aware of fire restrictions (if applicable), off-road travel restrictions, and camp at least 0.25 mile from paved roads and water sources.

Access

The North Rim is closed by snow each winter and is open from May 15 through October 15 only. To reach the North Rim from the east, follow U.S. Highway 89 south from Page, Arizona, for 25.8 miles, or take it 58.3 miles north from Cameron, Arizona, to the junction with US 89A. Follow US 89A north, then west, for 57.25 miles to Jacob Lake on the Kaibab Plateau at the junction with southbound Arizona Highway 67 (also known as the Kaibab Plateau–North Rim Parkway). Jacob Lake can also be reached from the north via US 89A, 29.8 miles south of the US 89A/AZ 389 junction in Fredonia, Arizona, and 34 miles south of US 89 in Kanab, Utah. The North Rim Entrance Station is 31 miles south of Jacob Lake via AZ 67. The road ends at Grand Canyon Lodge, 11.7 miles south of the entrance station.

7
KEN PATRICK TRAIL

General description: A half-day, round-trip day hike along the east rim of the Kaibab Plateau.

Distance: 6 miles round-trip.

Difficulty: Moderately easy.

Average hiking time: 3 to 4 hours round-trip.

Type of trail: Unmaintained; good condition.

Trailhead elevation: 8,819 feet.

Low point: 8,450 feet.

Elevation gain and loss: +360 feet; -730 feet.

Water availability: No water available.

Optimum season: Mid-May through mid-October.

Topo maps: USGS Point Imperial quad (trail not shown on map); Trails Illustrated Grand Canyon National Park.

Finding the trailhead: From the North Rim Entrance Station, proceed into the park for 9.5 miles to the junction with the Cape Royal/Point Imperial Road. Turn left and follow the narrow, winding pavement for 5.4 miles to a Y junction, then bear left toward Point Imperial. You will reach the Point Imperial parking area after another 2.7 miles.

The Ken Patrick Trail crosses the Cape Royal Road 1 mile from the Y junction. One-way hikers can shuttle a car or arrange for a pickup at a turnout 0.1 mile west of where the trail crosses the road.

Ken Patrick Trail

Key points:
0.0   Point Imperial parking area.
3.0   Cape Royal Road.

The hike: The Ken Patrick Trail stretches 10 miles across the Kaibab Plateau from Point Imperial to the North Kaibab trailhead, surveying cool Canadian Zone forests throughout its length. Only the 3-mile segment between Point Imperial and the Cape Royal Road follows the plateau rim. This segment of trail maintains mostly gentle grades, alternating from cool, shady conifer forests to openings that afford panoramic vistas into Nankoweap Creek canyon and beyond. This trip is an excellent choice for a summer day hike when searing heat envelops the inner Canyon. You need not hike the full 3 miles; the first mile of trail affords the finest vistas. Walk as far as you wish, find a good viewpoint, then relax and soak in the tremendous panoramas.

The trail begins at the west end of the Point Imperial parking area, the highest point reached by road in Grand Canyon National Park. A series of rock stairs leads you to the trail below, which begins a winding southwest course along the rim. Views from the beginning are dramatic, stretching past the slender Coconino Sandstone spire of Mount Hayden into the broad basin of Nankoweap Creek. Distant features in your view include Marble Canyon, the tortuous gorge of the Little Colorado River, Marble Platform, and the Painted Desert, stretching east to distant mesas that fade away into the desert haze. Even the San Francisco Peaks near Flagstaff are visible on the far southern horizon.

Your view also reaches south along the east rim of the Kaibab Plateau, where dense forest stretches far below onto slopes of the Toroweap Formation and Hermit Shale. An abundance of Rocky Mountain maple on those slopes enliven the somber forest with crimson foliage in early autumn.

The trail, only occasionally rocky, undulates along the rim for 0.4 mile, passing through a forest of ponderosa pine, Douglas-fir, white fir, and aspen. Gambel oak, manzanita, and New Mexican locust crowd sunny openings near the rim. After 0.4 mile, the trail abruptly descends 120 feet, via moderately steep switchbacks, into the shady confines of a narrow draw just below the Point Imperial Road. After it reaches the fir- and aspen-shaded floor of the draw, it descends briefly through thorny thickets of locust, then begins a steady, moderate ascent away from the road through the cool pine and fir forest to the next high point on the rim.

The pleasant trail next undulates generally southward, rising gently over minor hills and dropping slightly into saddles and shallow draws, staying a short distance west of the rim. En route you capture glimpses into Nankoweap Creek basin and the splintered buttes that punctuate its depths. Views to the northeast begin to open up as you proceed southward along the rim, reaching to Boundary Ridge, Marble Platform, the Echo Cliffs, and distant Navajo Mountain, a broad dome guarding invisible Glen Canyon in southern Utah.

As you gaze southward along the east rim of the plateau, you may notice various features that set this area apart from much of the rest of the Grand Canyon. The Kaibab

Limestone, which typically forms a broken cliff, has been subdued by erosion here into a steep slope, densely covered with conifer and aspen forest that extends unbroken down to the Coconino Sandstone. The east-facing slopes below you receive sunlight only during the morning and early afternoon hours, creating a microclimate that mimics conditions found on the plateau above. You will see tall conifers extending down to the Supai layer, and isolated groves that reach down to the base of the Redwall Limestone. In most places throughout the Grand Canyon, the Redwall separates the piñon-juniper woodland above from desert scrub communities below.

After 2.5 miles, the trail curves east to the last point affording views into Nankoweap basin, where a green ribbon of Fremont cottonwoods shades the perennial stream more than 5,000 feet below. From that point, you quickly descend to a saddle, then rise and fall in roller-coaster fashion over two forest-covered hills, finally reaching the rock stairway leading up to the Cape Royal Road at 8,480 feet after 3 miles. A rim trail, seldom used, continues south for another 3 miles to the parking area at Vista Encantadora (Vista Encantada on some maps). The Ken Patrick Trail, once nearly impassable due to blowdowns, has been brushed and cut out, mainly by volunteer trail crews, and now is easy to follow through the forest for another 7 miles to the North Kaibab trailhead.

If you have not managed to arrange a car shuttle to the one-vehicle turnout 250 yards west of the curve where the trail crosses the road, you will enjoy retracing your view-filled route back to Point Imperial.

8
CAPE FINAL

General description: A short but rewarding plateau-top day hike on the North Rim.

Distance: 4 miles round-trip.

Difficulty: Easy.

Average hiking time: 2 to 2.5 hours round-trip.

Type of trail: Rehabilitated dirt road; good condition.

Trailhead elevation: 7,847 feet.

High point: 8,000 feet.

Elevation gain: 150 feet.

Water availability: No water available.

Optimum season: Mid-May through mid-October.

Topo maps: USGS Walhalla Plateau quad; Trails Illustrated Grand Canyon National Park.

Finding the trailhead: Follow driving directions for Hike 7 to the Y junction with the Cape Royal Road, then bear right toward Cape Royal. You pass the crossing of the Ken Patrick Trail after 1 mile and the Vista Encantadora overlook after 4.6 miles. The small, easy-to-miss Cape Final trailhead lies on the left (east) side of the road 11.8 miles from the Y junction with the Point Imperial Rd. and 2.5 miles north of the road's end at Cape Royal.

Key points:

0.0 Cape Final Trailhead.

2.0 End of trail, west of Cape Final.

Cape Final

The hike: This trail offers the greatest rewards for the smallest investment of time and effort of any of the North Rim's plateau-top trails. The route follows a gently rising, long-closed road through parklike forests of ponderosa pine to a panoramic viewpoint on the east rim of the Kaibab Plateau, affording an unusual perspective from high above Unkar Creek canyon. This leisurely day hike is particularly attractive when summer heat grips the inner Grand Canyon.

From the trailhead, follow the signed Cape Final Trail east into the open forest of ponderosa pine. The trail rises gently and moderately to the crest of an 8,000-foot ridge after 0.75 mile, then follows an undulating course for another 0.5 mile through peaceful forest to a clearing at the rim of the plateau, where a dramatic view suddenly unfolds.

The depths of Chuar Valley spread out far below. Its broad lower reaches, where hills and gentle slopes are composed of soft Galeros Formation rocks (part of the Precambrian Grand Canyon Supergroup), contrast with the angular profile of the soaring cliffs above. Lava Creek, Chuar's western tributary, is bounded by a striking array of colorful buttes, including the square-edged crag of 7,914-foot Siegfried Pyre and the red, Supai-capped Gunther Castle. The deep, serpentine gorge of the Little Colorado River opens up beyond Marble Platform in the southeast, slicing through the platform into the distance.

From the overlook, sometimes used as a campsite, the trail bends south, then west, where piñons begin to supplant the ponderosa pines. The piñons, along with Gambel oak, sagebrush, cliffrose, and curl-leaf mountain mahogany, signal your approach to the rim, where an increase in available sunlight, thin soils, high evaporation, and hot, dry up-drafts from the Grand Canyon below create an environment inhospitable to ponderosa pine.

Soon the trail, more apparently an old road, curves back to the south, where it ends. A footpath winds a short distance through the piñon from there to the south rim of Cape Final, where a panoramic Grand Canyon vista unfolds. Far below lies Unkar Creek, with the bold pyramid of Vishnu Temple as a backdrop, winding through its cliff-bound canyon to broad Unkar Delta at the Colorado River. There the river silently flows through a comparatively wide valley, where long slopes of soft, red Dox Sandstone spread out on both sides of the river. Unkar Delta is notable not only for its size—some 300 acres—but also for the number of Anasazi dwelling sites discovered there by archaeologists. At least ninety-four sites, many with large rooms and some featuring kivas, suggest Anasazi occupation of Unkar Delta until the late twelfth century.

The vista encompasses a broad sweep of canyon landscapes. In the southeast your view reaches well into the shadowed gorge of the Little Colorado River and to the towering walls of the Palisades of the Desert, with the rolling hills of the Painted Desert stretching far into the distance beyond. Far to the south rises the Grand Canyon's South Rim, incised by a multitude of steep, short canyons plunging into the Colorado River gorge. Beyond the South Rim, the wooded expanse of the Coconino Plateau reaches out to the San Francisco volcanic field, punctuated by its namesake peaks, and to other lofty cones, such as Kendrick Peak and Bill Williams Mountain.

The actual point of Cape Final lies about 0.3 mile east of the overlook. Since it projects well into the void, it affords an all-encompassing view of lower Marble Canyon and the eastern Grand Canyon. You can reach Cape Final by a bushwhack route from the overlook, but perhaps the best way to reach it is to backtrack along the trail to the point where it first bends back to the north, about 200 yards beyond the margins of the piñon woodland. There, a faint path branches southeast from the main trail (the junction may be marked with a cairn); follow this path for about 150 yards through the ponderosa forest. Once this path begins to fade out, you can see Cape Final's Kaibab Limestone promontory up ahead. Simply weave a way through the piñon, Gambel oak, and curl-leaf mountain mahogany for another 0.2 mile or so to the point.

After enjoying this brief but rewarding hike, retrace your steps to the trailhead.

9
CLIFF SPRING

General description: A short but fascinating walk below the rim of Walhalla Plateau.

Distance: 1 to 2 miles round-trip.

Difficulty: Easy.

Average hiking time: 0.5 to 1 hour round-trip.

Type of trail: Unmaintained; good condition.

Trailhead elevation: 7,750 feet.

Low point: 7,500 feet.

Elevation loss: 150 to 200 feet.

Water availability: Cliff Spring requires treatment; bring your own water instead.

Optimum season: Mid-May through mid-October.

Topo maps: USGS Walhalla Plateau quad; Trails Illustrated Grand Canyon National Park.

Finding the trailhead: Follow driving directions for Hikes 7 and 8 to the Cape Final trailhead, then continue south on the Cape Royal Road for another 1.9 miles to the signed Cliff Spring trailhead, on the left (east) side of the road at Angels Window overlook. The trailhead lies 0.6 mile north of the road's end at Cape Royal and 13.7 miles south of the Point Imperial Road junction.

Key points:
0.0 Cliff Spring Trailhead.

0.5 Cliff Spring.
1.0 End of trail.

The hike: This trail is a fine, albeit brief, introduction to the plateau and rim environments of the North Rim. Distant views, a well-preserved Anasazi granary, and a dripping spring hidden in an alcove beneath the rim offer rewarding

Cliff Spring, Cape Royal

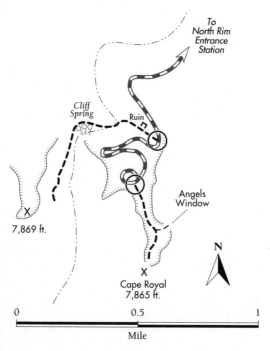

diversions for visitors budgeting their time and energy.

The brief stroll gets underway at the Angels Window overlook, which affords a fine view of that interesting natural opening in the Kaibab Limestone on the east rim of Cape Royal. Carefully cross the busy roadway and follow the wide gravel trail west down a shallow draw through the open forest of ponderosa pine. After only 100 yards, you will reach the ruins of a well-preserved Anasazi granary, hidden beneath a large Kaibab Limestone boulder. The Kayenta Anasazi who inhabited the Grand Canyon from A.D. 900 to A.D. 1150 were limited in numbers by the scant availability of water and arable land. Living in small bands, these people farmed in the canyons and atop the plateaus of the North Rim and stored their corn, beans, and squash in granaries such as this one.

Stroll down the draw beyond the ruin, descending a moderate grade into a larger draw joining on your right (north). Here, Douglas-fir joins the forest of ponderosa pine, and Gambel oaks gather in ranks on the slopes above. You soon cross the dry, rocky wash on the floor of the draw beneath spreading branches of boxelder, then follow a red ledge of Toroweap Formation rocks west. Walls of Kaibab Limestone overhang the ledge as you contour above the increasingly deep and rugged draw.

Seeps begin to emerge from the base of the Kaibab cliff, nurturing small clumps of mosses. Within moments you reach a deeper alcove where Cliff Spring emerges. Much like Dripping Spring on the South Rim (see Hike 6), numerous seeps converge here and drip steadily into shallow, mossy pools. Fine views, framed by scattered pines and

Douglas-firs, stretch southeast down the precipitous Clear Creek tributary below, past the erosion-isolated mesa of Wotans Throne to Kendrick Mountain and the San Francisco Peaks, nearly 60 miles distant.

The trail continues beyond the spring for 0.5 mile, offering a sampling of the nature of inner Canyon trails. The route beyond the spring is rough and rocky, undulating over and around obstacles such as boulders and trees. The trail follows the Toroweap ledge past another dripping spring, then bends south and descends along the western flanks of the plummeting canyon below. Here you may notice a change in the environment, since piñon, agave, Utah serviceberry, mormon tea, and roundleaf buffaloberry have supplanted the conifer forest due to the thin soils, southern exposure, and hot, dry updrafts from the canyon far below.

The Cape Royal peninsula rises boldly beyond the precipitous canyon to the southeast, bounded by cliffs of Kaibab Limestone and the buff-toned Coconino Sandstone, its cross-bedding preserving the great dunes of a vast desert that covered the region 270 million years ago. Vishnu Temple's pyramidal spire juts skyward above the Grand Canyon's vast gulf, beyond the narrow isthmus separating Cape Royal from Wotans Throne.

The trail ends in a shady slickrock alcove surrounded by red Toroweap Formation rocks. Don't attempt to follow the slickrock ledge around the point ahead—sheer cliffs plunge 1,000 feet. Be content with the view from the trail's end, then backtrack to the trailhead.

10
CAPE ROYAL

see map on page 56

General description: A short, easy walk to one of the North Rim's finest vista points.

Distance: 0.8 mile round-trip.

Difficulty: Easy.

Average hiking time: 0.5 hour round-trip.

Type of trail: Paved trail.

Trailhead elevation: 7,900 feet.

Low point: 7,865 feet.

Elevation loss: 35 feet.

Water availability: None available.

Optimum season: Mid-May through mid-October.

Topo maps: USGS Cape Royal quad; Trails Illustrated Grand Canyon National Park.

Finding the trailhead: Follow driving directions for Hikes 7, 8, and 9 to the Cliff Spring trailhead, then continue another 0.6 mile to the road's end at the Cape Royal parking area, 19.6 miles from the primary park road and 29.1 miles from the North Rim Entrance Station. Look for pit toilets and a picnic site at the parking area.

Key points:
0.0   Cape Royal parking area.
0.2   Junction with trail to Angels Window.
0.4   Cape Royal.

The hike: The promontory of Cape Royal, jutting southward into the Grand Canyon away from the North Rim, is a prominent landmark seen from many South Rim viewpoints. The point affords one of the canyon's more memorable vistas, and it is one of only two points on the North Rim offering views of the Colorado River. If you have only one day to spend on the North Rim, the short walk to Cape Royal should be at the top of your "must do" list.

The paved trail begins at the southeast corner of the parking area and leads south among a scattering of piñon and juniper and over the light gray Kaibab Limestone capping this part of the plateau. Interpretive signs along the way offer insights into the natural history of the area.

After 0.2 mile, the 150-yard path to Angels Window branches left, leading to one of the Grand Canyon's few arches. The trail ahead soon drops off the level of the wooded promontory to the viewpoint at Cape Royal, where a memorable vista unfolds. The wooded mesa of Wotans Throne, an erosional outlier of the North Rim, is separated from the cape by a knife-blade ridge. Its mesa stands guard over the yawning depths of Vishnu Creek canyon, to the south, and a precipitous tributary of Clear Creek, to the west. Vishnu Temple, Krishna Shrine, and an array of colorful, castlelike buttes rise boldly out of the great depths below.

Cliff bands of the Palisades of the Desert and the South Rim bound the opposite reaches of the Grand Canyon from east to southwest. Beyond the wooded fringe of the South Rim, some 60 miles distant, rise the lofty summits of the San Francisco Peaks and Kendrick Mountain.

From Cape Royal, retrace your steps to the trailhead.

11
WIDFORSS TRAIL

General description: A plateau-top half-day hike along a self-guided nature trail on the North Rim.
Distance: 4.2 miles round-trip.
Difficulty: Easy.
Average hiking time: 2 to 2.5 hours round-trip.
Type of trail: Unmaintained; good condition.
Trailhead elevation: 8,080 feet.
High point: 8,250 feet.
Elevation gain and loss: +250 feet; -150 feet.
Water availability: None available.
Optimum season: Mid-May through mid-October.
Topo maps: USGS Bright Angel Point quad; Trails Illustrated Grand Canyon National Park; Earthwalk Grand Canyon National Park or Bright Angel Trail.
Finding the trailhead: Follow driving directions for Hike 7 to the Cape Royal/Point Imperial Road junction and continue straight ahead; the sign points to visitor services. You will reach a sign showing the turnoff to Widforss Point after another 0.25 mile. Turn right here onto a good gravel road and skirt the margins of Harvey Meadow for another 0.6 mile to the signed trailhead on the left (west) side of the road.

Key points:
0.0   Widforss Trailhead.
2.1   Post 14, end of self-guiding segment of trail.

The hike: The Widforss Trail is arguably the finest plateau-top trail in Grand Canyon National Park. The route hugs the rim of The Transept, an abysmal tributary of Bright Angel Creek, as it passes splendid Grand Canyon viewpoints between shady stands of conifer and aspen. The mildly un-dulating trail is well-defined and easy to follow throughout its length. No water is available en route; be sure to pack an ample supply.

The trail and a point on the North Rim were named in honor of the artist Gunnar M. Widforss, the "painter of the national parks." Widforss spent much time in the 1920s and 1930s creating vivid watercolor images of the Grand Can-yon, his favorite national park. Fourteen numbered posts along the first 2.1 miles of the trail are keyed to a pamphlet available from a dispenser at the trailhead (though the pam-phlet inaccurately estimates the distance at 2.5 miles). Pick one up before heading out on the trail; it will enhance your enjoyment and understanding through insight into some of the natural features and processes found along the trail.

The trail begins along the fringes of Harvey Meadow, heading south among scattered groves of Engelmann spruce, white fir, ponderosa pine, and aspen. A pair of rocky switchbacks soon lead up and over exposures of Kaibab Limestone to the beginning of a lengthy traverse high above The Transept, a 4,000-foot-deep tributary canyon of Bright

Widforss Trail

To Jacob Lake

To Point Imperial; Cape Royal

To Point Sublime

N

0   0.5   1

Mile

RIM

NORTH

Widforss   Trail

Post #14

Grand Canyon Lodge

The Transept

Upper Upper Ribbon Falls

Oza Butte 8,068 ft.

Widforss Point 7,822 ft.

Angel Creek. François Matthes, a topographer with the U.S. Geographic Survey, declared in the early 1900s that The Transept was far grander than Yosemite Valley. Although you may not agree, The Transept is an impressive defile none-theless.

The trail bends in and out of seven minor draws, staying just north of the rim during the first 2.2 miles. At first you proceed above the headwaters draw of The Transept, where you can see a dense forest of spire-topped spruce and fir, reminiscent of a subalpine forest in the Rocky Mountains, on the north-facing slopes above it. Soon, that draw begins to plummet away into the gaping abyss of The Transept, as the trail proceeds west along the rim through a forest of ponderosa pine, white fir, and aspen. Engelmann spruce joins the forest only in the shadiest draws.

Typical of most rim trails, the route often stays away from the rim, so rather than a continuum of Grand Canyon vistas, you enjoy occasional tree-framed views from the points separating the draws en route. Long-range views extend down The Transept into the depths of Bright Angel Creek, bounded on the southeast by the towering buttes of Brahma and Zoroaster temples, and far beyond to the Coconino Plateau, its wooded expanse punctuated by Red Mountain, Kendrick Peak, the San Francisco Peaks, and Bill Williams Mountain.

At Post 14, after 2.1 miles, you've reached the end of the self-guided segment of the trail. The trail continues another 2.8 miles to the Widforss Point overlook, though to complete that rewarding hike requires a greater commitment of time and energy. From Post 14, backtrack to the trailhead.

12
UNCLE JIM TRAIL

General description: A plateau-top loop hike to a viewpoint on the North Rim.

Distance: 3.9 miles round-trip.

Difficulty: Moderately easy.

Average hiking time: 2 to 3 hours round-trip.

Type of trail: Unmaintained; good condition.

Trailhead elevation: 8,250 feet.

High point: 8,450 feet.

Elevation gain and loss: 600 feet.

Water availability: None available.

Optimum season: Mid-May through mid-October.

Topo maps: USGS Bright Angel Point quad; Trails Illustrated Grand Canyon National Park; Earthwalk Grand Canyon National Park or Bright Angel Trail.

Finding the trailhead: From Jacob Lake, Arizona, follow Arizona Highway 67 south for 31.2 miles to the North Rim Entrance Station, then continue south into the park. The park highway ahead winds through lovely meadows and forests of pine, fir, spruce, and aspen. You pass the Cape Royal/Point Imperial Road junction after 9.5 miles; continue straight ahead for another 0.9 mile, where a prominent sign indicates the Kaibab Trail parking lot on the left (east) side of the road.

This parking lot often fills to capacity nearly every day by late morning. If it is full when you arrive, you must drive to the public parking areas near Grand Canyon Lodge, then either walk the mule trail that parallels the park road for 1.5 miles to the trailhead or ride the shuttle bus. (Inquire at the Grand Canyon Lodge transportation desk for shuttle schedules.)

Key points:
0.0   North Kaibab Trailhead.
0.4   Junction with Ken Patrick Trail; bear right.
0.9   Junction with loop trail; bear left.
2.0   Uncle Jim Point overlook.
3.0   Return to junction with loop trail; bear left.
3.9   North Kaibab Trailhead.

The hike: Much like the longer Widforss Trail, the mildly undulating Uncle Jim Trail traverses cool Kaibab Plateau forests en route to a splendid Grand Canyon viewpoint. From trail's end hikers gain an excellent overview of Roaring Springs Canyon and can visually trace the route of the North Kaibab Trail as it winds its way from the North Rim to the Redwall Limestone.

The trail, waterless throughout its length, is rougher and rockier than other North Rim trails due to occasional mule traffic. Overnight camping is allowed on this route (with a backcountry use permit), making it a good choice for a short backpack when intense summer heat grips the inner Grand Canyon. Most hikers can complete this semi-loop hike in about two hours, but three hours allows for a more leisurely pace.

The trail was named in honor of James T. "Uncle Jim"

Uncle Jim Trail, North Kaibab Trail

Owens. Formerly a game warden in Yellowstone National Park, Owens was hired in 1906 by the Forest Service to serve as game warden in the Grand Canyon Game Reserve on the Kaibab Plateau. He lived part time in the cave near the Widforss Trailhead on the north edge of Harvey

Meadow. At the time, game management theories called for the elimination of "undesirable" predatory species in favor of "harmless" wildlife such as deer. By 1918, Uncle Jim claimed to have killed 532 mountain lions. The tragic result was the explosive growth of the Kaibab deer population, reaching an estimated 100,000 deer by 1924. The population was far greater than their limited range on the Kaibab Plateau could sustain, and thousands died of starvation during the hard winter of 1924-1925. Today we recognize that predators are more efficient game managers, and mountain lions thrive on the Kaibab Plateau.

Uncle Jim Owens did leave a better legacy to the Grand Canyon region. In 1906, he and others brought bison to the Kaibab Plateau. This herd was the progenitor of the herd that now occupies the House Rock Valley, and occasionally some of the approximately 125 bison range up into the plateau meadows.

The Uncle Jim and Ken Patrick trails begin as a single path from the east edge of the North Kaibab trailhead parking lot adjacent to the mule corral. At first, the trails follow the North Rim east through a forest of ponderosa pine and aspen, the trees' ranks opening enough to afford fine views into the rugged depths of Roaring Springs Canyon and, beyond, the South Rim and the distant San Francisco Peaks.

Soon you contour away from the rim, entering heavy forest dominated by white fir. The previously level trail dips into a minor draw, then gradually ascends to a signed junction at 8,300 feet, beneath a grove of stout, towering pines. Bear right here onto the Uncle Jim Trail. The tread becomes quite gravelly ahead as you descend a moderate grade northeast through mixed conifer forest into the shady confines of the headwaters draw of Roaring Springs Canyon. As you ascend a moderate grade out of the draw, Engelmann spruce makes a brief appearance among the pine, fir, and aspen on the sheltered northwest-facing slopes.

After ascending a few minor switchbacks, you then rise to an unsigned junction at 8,350 feet, where you are faced with the only decision you must make on this trip. This junction marks the beginning of a loop trail to Uncle Jim Point. Both legs of the loop reach the point and are about 1 mile long, but since the left leg leads to Grand Canyon views sooner, most hikers bear left at the junction. That leg of the loop ascends gently through peaceful forest.

After 0.3 mile you gain the top of a broad ridge at your high point of 8,450 feet, then begin a long curve toward the south. Soon the trail skirts the east rim of the ridge, where views open up into the cliff-bound depths of upper Bright Angel Canyon and beyond it to the flat, forested expanse of Walhalla Plateau. These features soon fade from view as you duck back into the forest and head southwest away from the rim.

About 1.1 miles from the loop trail junction, you meet the west leg of the loop joining from the north. Continue straight ahead, past a dilapidated mule hitching rail, and follow the path down over slabs of Kaibab Limestone out to the overlook, just below the rim at 8,300 feet. Here the rim effect is well pronounced. Piñon, juniper, cliffrose, and Utah serviceberry from the inner canyon share space with Gambel oak, ponderosa pine, and white fir, trees of the Kaibab Plateau high country.

Though your view is somewhat obstructed by the small trees and shrubs massed at the point, it reaches far below into the abyss of Roaring Springs Canyon, past its confluence with Bright Angel Canyon, to a high ridge capped by bold towers: Deva Temple, Hattan Butte, and Brahma and Zoroaster temples. The long-range view stretches 12 miles across the Grand Canyon to the South Rim and beyond. Look out across the thickly wooded expanse of the Coconino Plateau, punctuated by the summits of Red Butte near the town of Tusayan; 9,256-foot Bill Williams Mountain; 10,418-foot Kendrick Peak; and the lofty San Francisco Peaks. It's crowned by 12,633-foot Humphreys Peak, the highest point in Arizona.

The well-defined switchbacks of the North Kaibab Trail can be seen leading through the cliffs into Roaring Springs Canyon, and you can visually trace that trail through the Redwall Limestone into the canyon far below. To return to the trailhead, backtrack several yards to the junction and bear left onto the west leg of the loop. This pleasant but viewless trail mildly undulates through a forest of white fir, ponderosa pine, and aspen for 1 mile to the junction with the other leg of the loop. Bear left there and retrace your steps for 0.9 mile to the trailhead.

13
NORTH KAIBAB TRAIL TO SUPAI TUNNEL

see map on page 67

General description: A half-day hike below the rim, on the North Rim's only maintained inner canyon trail.

Distance: 3.6 miles round-trip.

Difficulty: Moderate.

Average hiking time: 3 to 4 hours, round-trip.

Type of trail: Maintained; excellent condition.

Trailhead elevation: 8,250 feet.

Low point: 6,840 feet.

Elevation loss: 1,410 feet.

Water availability: Piped drinking water is available May through October at Supai Tunnel. Always bring your own water to be safe in the event of a water pipeline break.

Optimum season: Mid-May through mid-October.

Topo maps: USGS Bright Angel Point quad; Trails Illustrated Grand Canyon National Park; Earthwalk Bright Angel Trail or Grand Canyon National Park.

Finding the trailhead: Follow driving directions for Hike 12.

Key points:
0.0   North Kaibab Trailhead.
1.8   Supai Tunnel.

The hike: The North Kaibab Trail is the North Rim's only maintained trail, lying within the frequently patrolled Cor-

71

ridor Zone of the park. Unlike many of the Grand Canyon's trails, which follow the path of least resistance in search of breaks in the cliff bands, this straightforward trail forges its way through obstructions. More hikers pound this trail than any other on the North Rim, for ample reasons. The tread is wide and only occasionally rocky, and it descends moderately rather than steeply. The way offers a classic sampling of all the life zones present in the Grand Canyon, and the landscapes it traverses and the views it affords are dramatic.

The 3.6-mile round-trip to Supai Tunnel offers memorable inner canyon views and a fine introduction to Grand Canyon hiking. The high elevations that the trail traverses are cooler in summer than other inner canyon trails, though temperatures can still be hot. A fine alternative to hiking all the way to Supai Tunnel is the 1.4-mile round-trip to the ledges atop the Coconino Sandstone, only 500 feet below the rim. The top of the Coconino affords unobstructed views into the yawning depths of Roaring Springs Canyon.

The trail begins behind the information sign at the rim, below the entrance to the trailhead parking lot. You descend steadily at once, passing through a cool forest of white fir, Douglas-fir, ponderosa pine, and aspen. The initial descent through Kaibab Limestone passes unnoticed, since erosion has subdued the Kaibab's typical cliff into a slope cloaked behind dense vegetation. Switchbacks soon lead you deeper into the void of Roaring Springs Canyon, and the grade abates briefly atop sheer, desert-varnished cliffs of Coconino Sandstone. Gnarled pines and firs clinging to the slickrock rim of the cliffs are reminiscent of a scene from Yosemite.

Conifers persist as you follow switchbacks through the

break in the Coconino. A wide variety of shrubs dress these slopes and the red slopes of Hermit Shale below. En route the trail forges a way through thickets of Rocky Mountain maple, Gambel oak, mallow ninebark, elderberry, thorny New Mexican locust, wild rose, and silktassel. An occasional juniper infiltrates the ranks of Douglas-fir and white fir that dominate the shady slopes.

After 1.8 miles, at 6,840 feet, you reach a water faucet offering seasonal water and toilets in a confined, rocky draw. Just ahead at the portal of Supai Tunnel is a passageway through the Esplande Sandstone. From the confines of the shady draw, retrace your steps to the trailhead.

14

TRANSEPT TRAIL

General description: A pleasant walk through the forest along the North Rim.

Distance: 1.7 miles one way; 3.4 miles round-trip.

Difficulty: Easy.

Average hiking times: 45 minutes to 1 hour one way; 1.5 to 2 hours round-trip.

Type of trail: Unmaintained; good condition.

Trailhead elevations: 8,300 feet at the campground; 8,200 feet at the lodge.

Elevation gain and loss: 100 feet.

Water availability: Available at the campground.

Optimum season: Mid-May through mid-October.

Topo maps: USGS Bright Angel Point quad; Trails Illustrated Grand Canyon National Park; Earthwalk Bright Angel Trail or Grand Canyon National Park.

Finding the trailhead: This trail links Grand Canyon Lodge with the North Rim Campground. Follow driving directions for Hike 13 to the Kaibab Trailhead, and continue straight ahead along the primary park road for another 2.3 miles to the spacious public parking lots located on the left (east) side of the road just before it ends at Grand Canyon Lodge.

To reach the campground, turn right at the prominently signed campground road 1.2 miles north of the lodge, or 11.5 miles south of the North Rim Entrance Station, and drive 0.3 mile to the campground. The trail begins next to the general store near the campground entrance. Spur trails also connect the campground with the Transept Trail.

Key points:
0.0   Grand Canyon Lodge.
1.7   North Rim Campground.

The hike: This trail is most frequently used by campground guests as a connection to Grand Canyon Lodge. Yet day hikers can still use the trail, though they must park in the public parking lots at the lodge. From there, find the trail by following the Bright Angel Point Trail to the lodge and turn right, or simply walk through the lodge and find the trail below the patio.

The Transept Trail is smooth and generally level, except for a 100-foot descent (or ascent, depending upon your direction of travel) in the first 0.4 mile from the campground. The trail passes through cool forests of pine, fir, and aspen, as it bends into four minor draws along the rim of The Transept, a prominent tributary canyon of Bright Angel Creek. Due to moderate forest cover, hikers will enjoy only occasional glimpses into the 3,200-foot trench of The Transept.

Transept Trail, Bright Angel Point

To North Rim Entrance Station,
Jacob Lake

To Point
Imperial,
Uncle Jim
Point

Ranger Station,
Backcountry
Office

Fuel

Showers,
Laundry

General
Store

North
Rim
Campground

To
Cottonwood
Campground,
Phantom Ranch

Transept Trail

N

The Transept

Grand Canyon
Lodge

Bright Angel
Point

0   0.5   1

Mile

15
BRIGHT ANGEL POINT

see map on page 76

General description: A short walk leading to a dramatic vista point on the North Rim.

Distance: 0.8 mile round-trip.

Difficulty: Easy.

Average hiking time: 0.5 hour round-trip.

Type of trail: Paved trail.

Trailhead elevation: 8,240 feet.

Low point: 8,150 feet.

Elevation loss: 90 feet.

Water availability: None available.

Optimum season: Mid-May through mid-October.

Topo maps: USGS Bright Angel Point quad; Trails Illustrated Grand Canyon National Park; Earthwalk Bright Angel Trail or Grand Canyon National Park.

Finding the trailhead: Follow driving directions for Hike 13 to the Kaibab Trailhead, then continue straight ahead along the primary park road for another 2.3 miles to the spacious public parking lots located on the left (east) side of the road just before it ends at Grand Canyon Lodge.

Key points:

0.0   Grand Canyon Lodge public parking area.

0.2   Junction with trail from lodge; continue straight ahead.

0.4   Bright Angel Point.

The hike: Grand Canyon Lodge, at road's end on the North Rim, is the focal point for the majority of visitors to this remote part of Grand Canyon National Park. While you're here enjoying the comforts of the lodge or simply visiting for the day, don't miss the short and easy stroll to Bright Angel Point, an overlook that affords one of the most dramatic views of the Grand Canyon from the North Rim. There are few better places to enjoy an incomparable canyon sunrise or sunset.

Day-use visitors will find the trail behind the log shelter at the public parking lot. Guests staying at the lodge can find the trail below the east patio behind the lodge. Pamphlets describing this self-guided nature trail are available from the dispenser at the log shelter.

From the public parking lot, follow the trail as it leads south between the rim of Roaring Springs Canyon and the lodge cabins. After 250 yards, the trail from the lodge joins on your right (0.1 mile from the lodge itself). The trail ahead follows the crest of a narrow Kaibab Limestone promontory among scattered piñon and juniper for another 0.3 mile to the 8,150-foot viewpoint, where a breathtaking vista unfolds. A score of colorful buttes, the mile-deep trough of the Grand Canyon, and the soaring battlements of the South Rim spread out in an explosion of color and form. The gaping trench of Bright Angel Creek lies virtually at your feet, its bottom 4,000 feet below. You can visually trace that arrow-straight canyon far into the depths of the Grand Canyon and beyond to the South Rim. On the far southern horizon rise the lofty highlands of the San Francisco Peaks, Kendrick Mountain, Red Mountain, and Bill Williams Mountain.

From the point, return the way you came.

16

NORTH BASS TRAIL TO MUAV CABIN

General description: A half-day hike from a remote North Rim trailhead to a historic cabin below the rim.

Distance: 2 miles round-trip.

Difficulty: Moderate.

Average hiking time: 2.5 hours round-trip.

Type of trail: Unmaintained; fair condition.

Trailhead elevation: 7,520 feet.

Low point: 6,700 feet.

Elevation loss: 820 feet.

Water availability: None available.

Optimum season: Late May or early June through mid-October.

Topo maps: USGS King Arthur Castle quad; Trails Illustrated Grand Canyon National Park.

Finding the trailhead: From Jacob Lake, Arizona, follow Arizona Highway 67 south for 26.5 miles to the prominently signed junction with Forest Road 22 (also signed for Dry Park 10) and turn right (west). This junction lies 0.9 mile south of Kaibab Lodge and immediately south of tiny Deer Lake. This good gravel road, with washboards, ascends steadily through spruce, fir, and aspen forest for 2.1 miles to the signed junction with FR 270, where you turn left (south). Follow this occasionally rough and rocky road for 2.3 miles, avoiding two unsigned right-forking roads en route, to a junction where a sign points west to Fire Point 12. Turn right here onto FR 223, also rough and rocky in places, and proceed 5.8 miles to left-branching FR 268, signed for Swamp Point, your destination.

Follow FR 268 south; it's rough and rocky in places. After 0.3 mile, turn left onto FR 268B, a good but narrow gravel road. Follow FR 268B for 1.2 miles to the national park boundary, where the road is designated W4, and its condition quickly deteriorates. Rocks, roots, potholes, and, farther on, high centers make the use of a high-clearance vehicle advisable. After driving 0.2 mile from the park boundary, avoid an unsigned road that branches left to Kanabownits Spring, and bear right, proceeding generally west through the pristine forest of pine, fir, and aspen. You will pass an inviting camping/parking area 7.8 miles from the park boundary, after which the road becomes extremely rough and rocky for the final 0.1 mile to the Swamp Point trailhead, 19.6 miles from AZ 67.

Hikers arriving late in the day can camp wherever they wish along the access roads within Kaibab National Forest. You can camp at the Swamp Point trailhead only after obtaining a permit from the Backcountry Reservations Office (Use Area NJ9, Swamp Ridge).

Note: The final segment of the road to Swamp Point, within park boundaries, is blocked each winter by fallen trees. National Park Service fire crews may not clear the road until mid-June or later each year. Remember that park regulations prohibit driving off established roadways. Consult park rangers regarding road conditions before driving this road.

Key points:
0.0   Swamp Point Trailhead.
1.0   Trail junction at Muav Saddle; turn right and descend to Muav Cabin.

The hike: Historic Muav Cabin rests in a pine grove just north of Muav Saddle, a prominent notch separating the North Rim from isolated Powell Plateau. The cabin is easily reached via the best segment of the North Bass Trail, one of the most difficult and demanding trails in the Grand Canyon. This trail, an old Indian route once known as the Shinumo Trail (*shinumo* is a Paiute word referring to the ancient cliff-dwelling inhabitants of the canyon), was later improved by a prospector known only as White, who may have lived for a time near the spring near Muav Saddle. William Wallace Bass, who constructed the South Bass Trail in the 1880s, rebuilt the so-called White Trail to the North Rim by 1900. Using a cable crossing at the Colorado River, Bass guided tourists from the South Rim to the North Rim via his trail, some on sightseeing trips, others on hunting trips.

Much of the scenery en route is quite different from any other area in the Grand Canyon. Erosion along the Muav Fault has softened the abrupt edges of the North Rim and upper Muav Canyon, which has a broad, V-shaped profile. Soils in Muav Canyon are well developed, and dense brush forms a perpetually green veneer that masks the broken, rocky slopes.

From road's end at Swamp Point, the trail follows a series of switchbacks on a moderately descending grade via the steep slopes west of the point. Views from the begin-

North Bass Trail to Muav Cabin

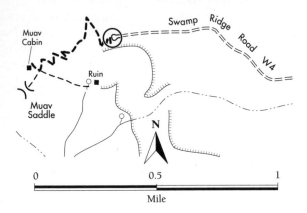

ning are excellent, stretching northwest across the wooded red rock platform of The Esplanade into broad Tapeats Amphitheater. The slopes below the point were charred in a 1989 fire, and now, among the blackened snags of piñon and juniper, the slopes have been reclaimed by thickets of Gambel oak, silktassel, and Utah serviceberry.

As the rocky switchbacks lead you closer to Muav Saddle, hikers exchange views of Tapeats Amphitheater for views down the deep, brushy trough of Muav Canyon to an array of colorful buttes and the distant South Rim. Muav Cabin comes into view, nestled in a shady grove of ponderosa pines, as you approach the saddle. After 1 mile you will reach an unmarked junction in the deep notch of Muav Saddle amid a thicket of Gambel oak at 6,711 feet. Trails lead straight ahead to Powell Plateau, right to Muav Cabin, and left to Muav Canyon. Turn right and descend several yards to the cabin.

Muav Cabin, built as a patrol cabin by the National Park Service in 1925, lies several yards north of the saddle via a well-worn path. President Theodore Roosevelt camped near the site while hunting mountain lions in 1903, hence the cabin is sometimes called Teddy's Cabin. The structure, with two rooms and cots, is in remarkably good condition. After contemplating the cabin's history and enjoying the region's quiet beauty, backtrack to the trailhead.

17
BILL HALL TRAIL TO MONUMENT POINT

General description: An easy, short hike to a remote North Rim viewpoint overlooking the central Grand Canyon.
Distance: 1.6 miles round-trip.
Difficulty: Easy.
Average hiking time: 1 hour round-trip.
Type of trail: Unmaintained; fair to good condition.
Trailhead elevation: 7,050 feet.
Low point: 7,030 feet.
High point: 7,206 feet.
Elevation gain and loss: +175 feet; -60 feet.
Water availability: None available.
Optimum season: Mid-May through mid-October.
Topo maps: USGS Tapeats Amphitheater quad; Trails Illustrated Grand Canyon National Park.
Finding the trailhead: Although the driving distance to the Bill Hall trailhead is longer than any other in Grand Canyon National Park, the gravel roads are in very good condition, and the 1.5-hour trip from the highway is an enjoyable scenic drive through the rich forests of the Kaibab Plateau.

From Jacob Lake, Arizona, follow Arizona Highway 67 south for 26.5 miles to the junction with Forest Road 22 (also signed for Dry Park 10) and turn right (west). This junction lies 0.9 mile south of Kaibab Lodge and immediately south of tiny Deer Lake. All junctions ahead are well-signed. Stay on FR 22 (sometimes signed Forest Road 422) for 17.6 miles, then turn left onto FR 425, signed for Thunder River Trail 13. After another 7.7 miles, avoid right-branching FR 233 (signed for Wilderness Trails); it leads to trailheads on the fringes of the Kanab Creek Wilderness. After another 0.6 mile, also avoid right-branching FR 232, signed for Thunder River Trail 5; it leads to the Indian Hollow trailhead. Stay left at that junction, remaining on FR 425, signed for Crazy Jug Point 4.

Continue straight ahead for another 1.7 miles (10 miles from FR 22), where FR 425 branches left and becomes a poor, unmaintained road at a junction adjacent to the Big Saddle Cabin and corrals. Bear right here, staying on the good gravel road, now FR 292. Bear right again after 0.25 mile and follow signs pointing to Crazy Jug Point. Soon you will reach a four-way junction atop the North Rim, 1.5 miles from FR 425. Follow the middle fork, FR 292A, a smooth but narrow dirt road, for the remaining 1.7 miles to the spacious trailhead parking area at road's end, 30.8 miles from the highway.

All roads en route to the trailhead lie within the boundaries of the Kaibab National Forest. Hikers arriving late in the day can camp wherever they wish along the route.

Key points:
0.0   Bill Hall Trailhead.
0.8   Monument Point.

The hike: This trip combines a satisfying scenic drive through the rich conifer forests of the Kaibab Plateau with a short hike to remote Monument Point. Vistas from the point survey a broad panorama of the central Grand Canyon, a landscape viewed by only a handful of visitors each year, and one far different from more familiar scenes in the eastern Grand Canyon. The trail also passes through the wake of a lightning-caused fire that charred thousands of acres of forest and woodland on the western reaches of the Kaibab Plateau in spring 1996. As early as the fall of that year, grasses were reclaiming the charred ground, and Gambel oaks were vigorously sending out new branches from their root crowns. Charred snags of piñon and juniper remind hikers of the rich woodland that once thrived here, a woodland that will likely take many generations to regenerate.

From the trailhead, pass through a gate in an old fenceline, avoid a right-branching forest road, and follow the trail to the left, indicated by National Park Service signs. Within moments, the trail leads down to a saddle on the rim, where it forks. The right branch is the main trail; the left branch leads a short distance to a point offering a fine view of Tapeats Amphitheater. On the point is a plaque placed in memory of Ward "Bill" Hall, for whom the trail was named.

Beyond this detour, the Bill Hall Trail begins a moderate ascent of the hill ahead, passing through a charred woodland of piñon and juniper. After topping the hill at 7,206 feet, the trail angles briefly downhill, then gently ascends the rim to turn south just east of Monument Point. Backpackers en route to Thunder River and Deer Creek will continue following the trail. Those who wish to reach Monu-

Bill Hall Trail to Monument Point

ment Point should leave the trail here and walk about 75 yards up to the 7,166-foot point for a rewarding panorama. Fine vistas extend northwest across the vast tableland of the Kanab Plateau to the distant Vermilion Cliffs. Views into the Grand Canyon open up below and to the south. The slickrock expanse of Tapeats Amphitheater spreads out far below, surrounded by Muav Saddle, Powell Plateau, Steamboat Mountain, and Bridgers Knoll. Great Thumb Mesa looms boldly on the South Rim, separated from your vantage point by the 6-mile-wide void of the Grand Canyon.

Your view also stretches far away to the southwest down

the trough of the central Grand Canyon. Sheer cliffs of Redwall Limestone embrace the deep inner gorge. These cliffs are flanked on both sides by the extensive red sandstone platform of The Esplanade. The forested hills of mounts Logan and Trumbull define the western horizon. After enjoying the memorable vistas, retrace your steps to the trailhead.

About the Author

Ron Adkison, an avid hiker and backpacker, began his outdoor explorations at age six. Since then he has logged more than 8,000 trail miles in ten Western states. He has walked every trail in this guide to provide precise, firsthand information about the trails, as well as features of ecological and historical interest. When he's not on the trail, Ron lives on his family's mountain ranch and with the help of his wife, Lynette, and two children, Ben and Abbey, raises sheep and llamas.

Ron shares his love for the backcountry in this, his seventh guidebook.

HIKING GUIDES

BEST EASY DAY HIKES